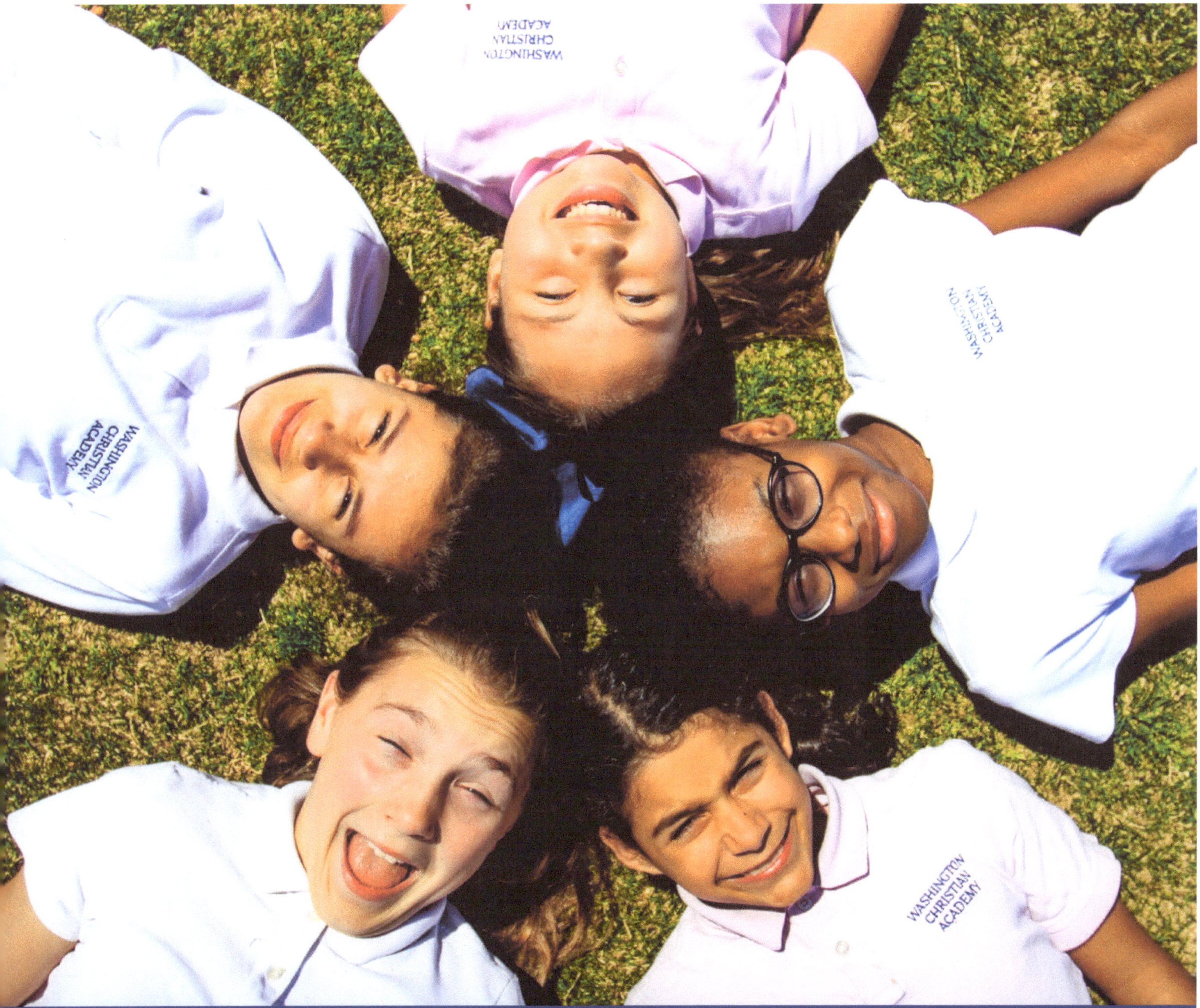

THE ULTIMATE GUIDE TO
SCHOOL MARKETING STRATEGIES

THE ULTIMATE GUIDE TO
SCHOOL MARKETING STRATEGIES

© 2017 All Rights Reserved

Schola Inbound Marketing
55 New Rd. Unit J6
Ephrata, PA 17522
www.schoolinboundmarketing.com

THE ULTIMATE GUIDE TO SCHOOL MARKETING STRATEGIES

ABOUT THE AUTHOR

Ralph Cochran is a fifteen-year veteran of implementing marketing and development growth strategies for Christian schools, universities and ministries. He is President of Schola, an inbound marketing agency committed to helping Christian schools grow enrollment. Due to his vast experience, Ralph has a reputation of correctly assessing a client's situation and bringing an effective solution to the table. His fresh and practical ideas have increased enrollment and retention while growing revenue and fundraising at Christian Schools. He is passionate about helping schools overcome the "gap" in their budget through strategically growing enrollment in order that a school can become financially sustainable.

He and the Schola team currently assist a number of schools and businesses as a retained consultant with their marketing, sales, and strategic planning for growth and sustained profitability. Ralph is also an avid speaker and loves listening to others' views and experiences. He understands that marketing is not about creating pretty brochures, clever sounding radio ads, or expensive billboards. When properly implemented, a sound marketing strategy is about attracting the right students to a school by re-positioning the school's brand as a thought leader in the community. Ultimately attracting the right students is about fulfilling the school's mission and getting children the best Christian education to build a legacy of Christian leaders to influence our country, churches, and families. And advancing toward this goal all begins with growing awareness of these schools and marketing their unique appeal to mission appropriate parents and students.

THE ULTIMATE GUIDE TO SCHOOL MARKETING STRATEGIES

Understanding Inbound Marketing to Successfully Grow Your School

THE ULTIMATE GUIDE TO SCHOOL MARKETING STRATEGIES

MARKETING FOR SCHOOLS

As the Head of a private Christian school, your passion is for the education and formation of children and teenagers. You have been given a mission and unique vision for the education of children. Your focus is rightfully directed toward the pedagogy, classroom management and curriculum that your school will use to fulfill its mission. Your interests probably do not lay in developing marketing strategies for your school. In fact, marketing and admission may be a real source of stress and anxiety for you.

You are not a marketing expert, and making important decisions about how to spend your limited marketing budget can be very difficult and even frustrating. Further, what is at stake in these decisions is of the utmost importance to the survival of your school. If you cannot find a way to create a steady stream of prospective families who look at your school and enroll, then it will be difficult to keep the doors open. It is of vital importance for you and the other leaders of your school to get a handle on what is involved in successfully marketing your school in the community.

As a school leader, the first thing that you need to know about marketing is that it is undergoing a seismic shift. The internet is profoundly affecting how businesses, organizations, and institutions interact with their customers and clients. It is not just that people are spending more dollars on internet advertising but that the strategies and tactics that are being deployed are profoundly different. In traditional marketing, you use a wide variety of media to shout your message out to the

THE ULTIMATE GUIDE TO SCHOOL MARKETING STRATEGIES

public and hope that some people in your target audience get it. I like to call this spray and pray marketing.

With the increased accessibility to the internet, a new approach, known as *inbound marketing*, is emerging. People are using the internet to search for information via their desktop, laptop, tablets, and smartphones. Through their searches, they are raising their hand and indicating their interest in your school. You have to be able to respond to these queries effectively with your website and social media presence.

The purpose of this guide is to help you become educated and informed so that you can develop an effective and current marketing plan for your school.

THE ULTIMATE GUIDE TO SCHOOL MARKETING STRATEGIES

Many Christian schools are established and successful. They may have an administrator dedicated to development and marketing as well as a significant marketing budget. However, if you are spending this marketing money on traditional marketing tactics like direct mailings and outdoor advertising that are not providing you the high enrollment that you desire, then you may be able to use this money more effectively and generate even more interest in your school for your marketing dollars.

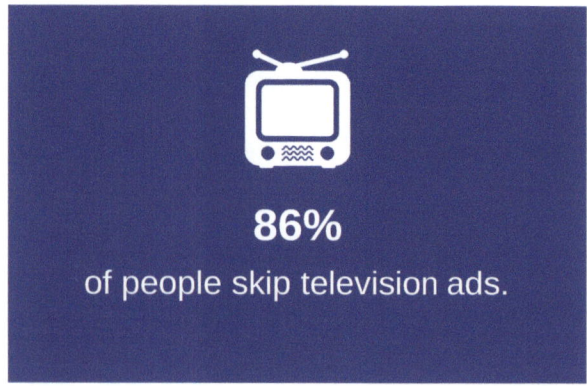

If you are involved in a school that is just starting out, you may not have the funds available to devote to marketing. The effectiveness of inbound marketing is good news for you. It is much less expensive to implement a simple inbound marketing strategy than it is to use traditional means of advertising. You may have to put in a lot of time initially and reallocate funds to establish this marketing program, but it will not add huge expenses to your tight budget.

TRADITIONAL MARKETING STRATEGIES ARE NO LONGER EFFECTIVE

The first thing you need to realize about marketing in today's world is that traditional marketing strategies and tactics are not producing the same results as they were five to ten years ago.

THE ULTIMATE GUIDE TO SCHOOL MARKETING STRATEGIES

Imagine Jill and Doug, Christian parents of three children and residing in the Washington DC and Baltimore suburbs. They know they have educational options and might be interested in a private school.

If you have invested heavily in traditional marketing, you may never reach them. Here's why:

- Jill and Doug don't subscribe to the town newspaper. The ad you purchased for your school open house will be ineffective.

- They tend to recycle the direct mails pieces that come to their home, so your beautifully designed postcard will likely wind up in the trash.

- As far as television, people like Jill and Doug record most programs and fast forward through the commercials. They are not going to see your expensive advertisement.

- In the car, Jill and Doug, like many young people today, listen to music from their playlist on their smartphone. They will not hear your radio advertisement.

- When Jill and Doug are driving around town, the billboards are going by far too fast for them to stop and write down the information to contact your school.

- Further, when Jill and Doug see your advertising, they may not be in a position to respond at that moment. They may forget to respond or lose the information. Your message does not reach them when they are ready to hear it.

TRADITIONAL ADVERTISING IS NOT TARGETED

You can see from our example that traditional advertising is not targeted to your ideal clients. The approach of most traditional advertising is to cast a wide net and to spray and pray based on the demographic profile of the audience. For example, only a small percentage of people that hear your radio advertisement will be in your target market. The hope is that if enough people hear the message, a few in the target market will respond. The more effective you can be at reaching your target group, the more success you will see in your marketing efforts.

TRADITIONAL ADVERTISING IS NOT EFFECTIVE

Most people today are just like Jill and Doug. They have successfully found ways to filter out much of the traditional forms of advertising that are attempting to reach them. In today's competitive marketplace, with so many different messages coming in, the claims of most traditional advertisements are suspect. People, like Jill and Doug, are looking for better and more trustworthy sources of information to solve their problems. They know they are not going to find this in a direct mailer or radio ad. When you pay for traditional advertising, you are shouting your message far and wide. The problem is that few people in your target market are listening anymore.

Traditional advertisements interrupt people when they are going about their daily lives. People do not like to be interrupted. You want to invest in a marketing strategy that draws people to you. Then you will not be disturbing them, but helping them to solve their problems.

TRADITIONAL ADVERTISING IS EXPENSIVE

Many small Christian schools have a limited budget for marketing. Marketing studies show that traditional methods are much more expensive than the newer Internet methods. The cost of a single lead using traditional marketing methods can be $350, while Internet marketing often costs as low as $125 per lead. You will have to collect your own data to measure how effective your marketing is, but it is safe to say that you will generate more high quality leads for your money with inbound marketing.

THE SOLUTION: INBOUND MARKETING

If traditional marketing is no longer effective, then what strategy does work? To answer this question, we can return to Jill and Doug, our Christian parents. They have a problem. They want to provide the best possible education for their children. In addition, they also want to make sure that faith is an important component of their children's lives. They are hungry for information about different educational options and for perspectives about how to pass on their faith to their children.

Where are they going to find the information that will help them solve their problem? One source is going to be through their relationships. They can ask their friends how they solved these same problems. However, Jill and Doug, like many of today's parents, are also going to search the Internet for information and opinions about the solution to their quandary. Here is how:

THE ULTIMATE GUIDE TO SCHOOL MARKETING STRATEGIES

- First, Jill and Doug go to a search engine website and enter some relevant keywords. In this case, they might enter "best Christian schools in Virginia."

- The search engine compiles a list of websites that might provide information related to this query using its algorithm for effectively sorting and ranking sites.

- Jill and Doug are offered a list of websites to view based on their inquiry. The top few sites are usually advertisements for organizations that have paid the search engine to appear in the results for relevant keyword searches. The other sites are known as the organic results because they are produced by the natural operation of the search algorithm.

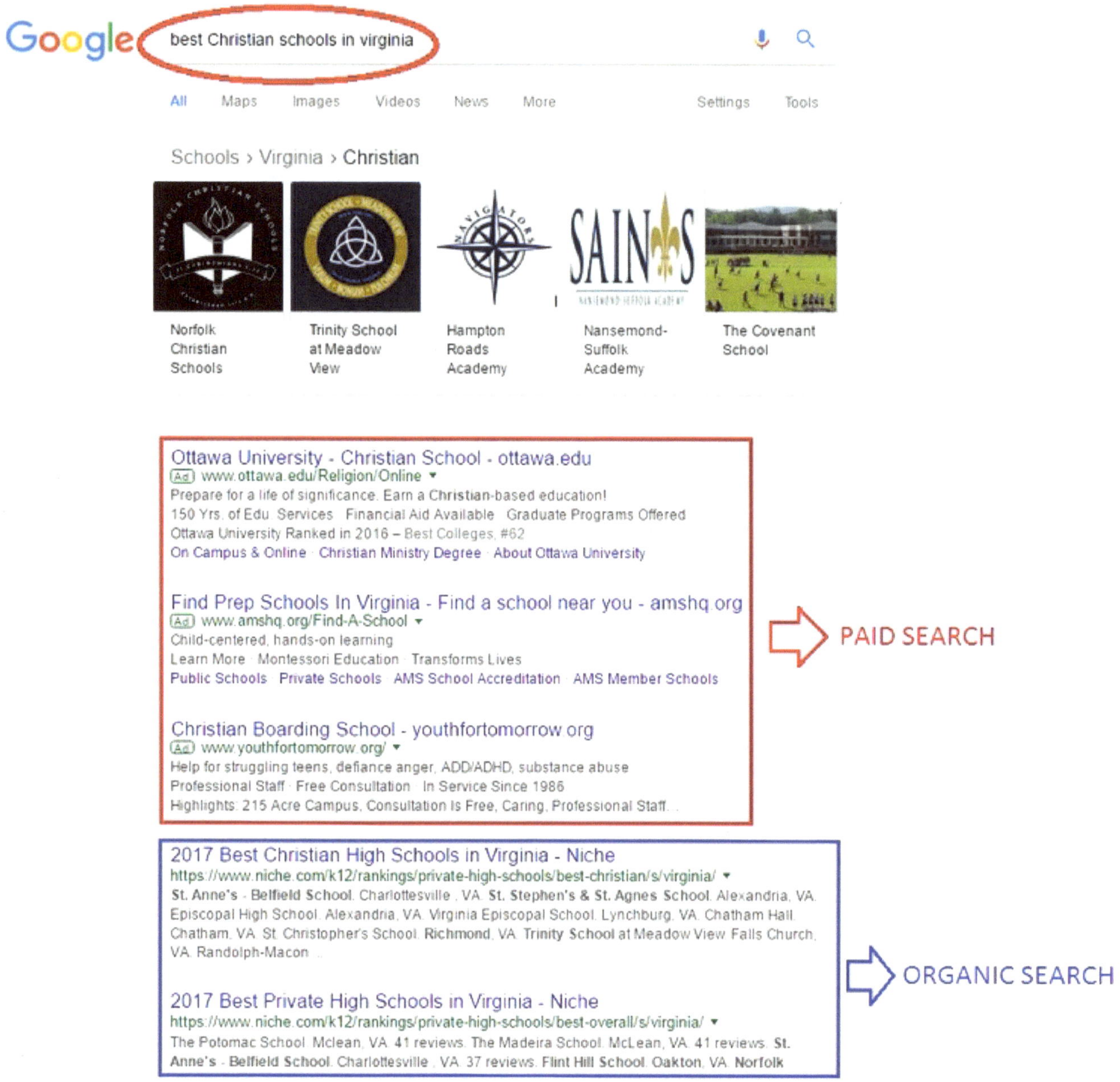

THE ULTIMATE GUIDE TO SCHOOL MARKETING STRATEGIES

- By clicking through and visiting different sites, Jill and Doug can find some relevant information about the best Christian schools in Virginia.

- Some sites may be very attractive, but are little more than trifold brochures in cyberspace that promote the school. They do not offer Jill and Doug much information to solve their problem. It is unlikely that Jill and Doug will follow up with schools that have websites like this.

- Other sites offer rich and robust content, not just about the school itself, but about how to make educational choices for Christian children in general. For example, Jill and Doug come across the website for Virginia Christian Academy that offers an active blog, podcasts and video content directed at helping Christian parents be more involved in their children's education.

THE ULTIMATE GUIDE TO SCHOOL MARKETING STRATEGIES

- The information that Jill and Doug find on this site is so valuable, that they connect with Virginia Christian's social media sites and continue to look forward to receiving information from the school.

- Eventually, Jill and Doug will come to trust Virginia Christian Academy as an expert in Christian education, after receiving relevant, timely, and meaningful emails that continue to grow their respect in the Academy.

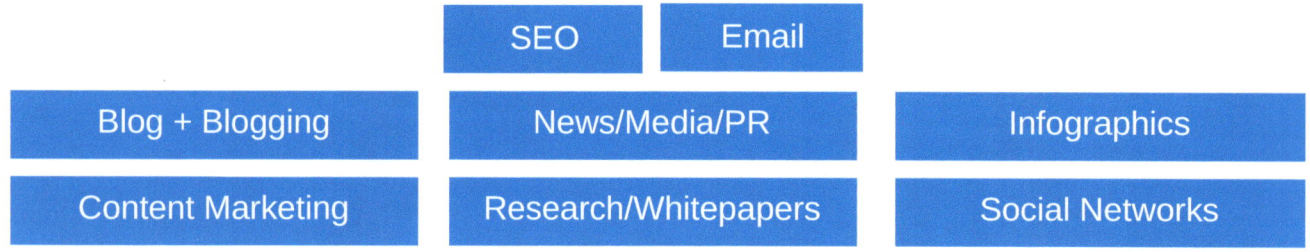

INBOUND MARKETING
AKA all the "free" traffic sources

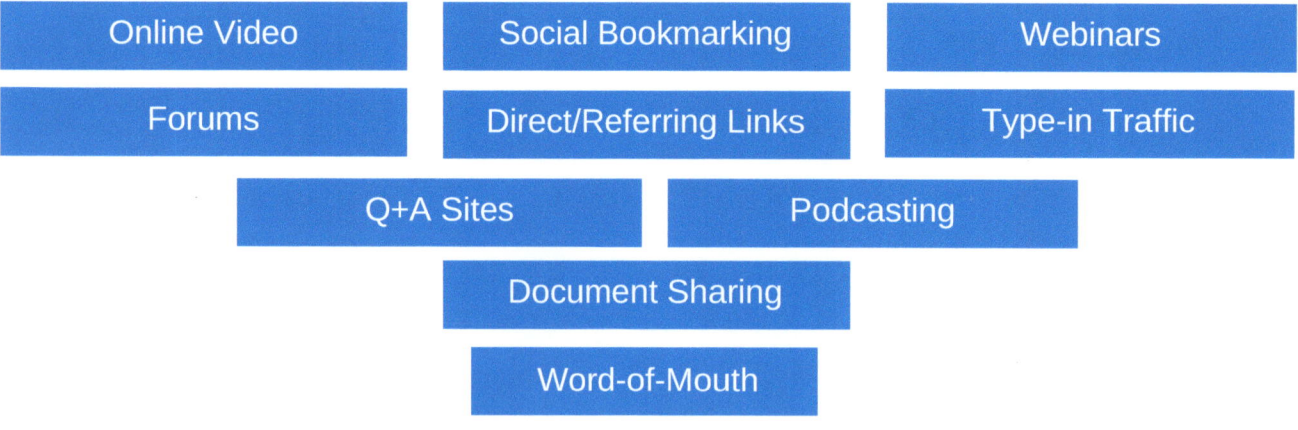

THE ULTIMATE GUIDE TO SCHOOL MARKETING STRATEGIES

- Often when this happens, they will submit their contact information to the school and arrange a visit to the campus or receive a well-timed phone call from the admissions staff inviting them to visit.

- Jill and Doug visit Virginia Christian Academy where they find a warm and welcoming staff. They are impressed by their classroom visits, and it is highly likely that they will apply for admission. Their experience of the school lines up with their expectations based on their experience of Virginia Christian Academy's web presence.

The kind of marketing employed by Virginia Christian Academy in this example is known as inbound marketing. It is a powerful alternative to traditional forms of marketing.

INBOUND MARKETING IS TARGETED

Virginia Christian Academy can target parents like Jill and Doug. Through their use of search engines, Jill and Doug have identified themselves as having a specific problem. Virginia Christian Academy designed its website so that it appears prominently in the list of results for the internet searches that Jill and Doug conducted to solve their problem. Virginia Christian Academy attracts many parents just like Jill and Doug, who are confronting the same set of problems and issues.

INBOUND MARKETING IS EFFECTIVE

You can see in our example that Virginia Christian Academy is effective in getting its message across to Christian parents like Jill and Doug. By presenting itself as an expert adviser, Jill and Doug come to trust Virginia Christian Academy as they make their decision about the education for their children.

THE ULTIMATE GUIDE TO SCHOOL MARKETING STRATEGIES

While they filter out most traditional advertising, Jill and Doug are seeking out the information and content that Virginia Christian is publishing. Instead of trying to interrupt Jill and Doug, Virginia Christian provides helpful information for them to solve problems. This information is available all day long so Jill and Doug can access it when they are thinking about solving their problem.

INBOUND MARKETING IS LESS EXPENSIVE

While there are costs involved in inbound marketing, effective digital marketing campaign will cost much less than traditional forms of marketing. There are no expensive mailing pieces to design and send also no billboards to rent or expensive advertisements to buy. Maintaining an effective web and social media presence is far less expensive than most traditional advertising. It does require time and attention, but it need not cost a fortune.

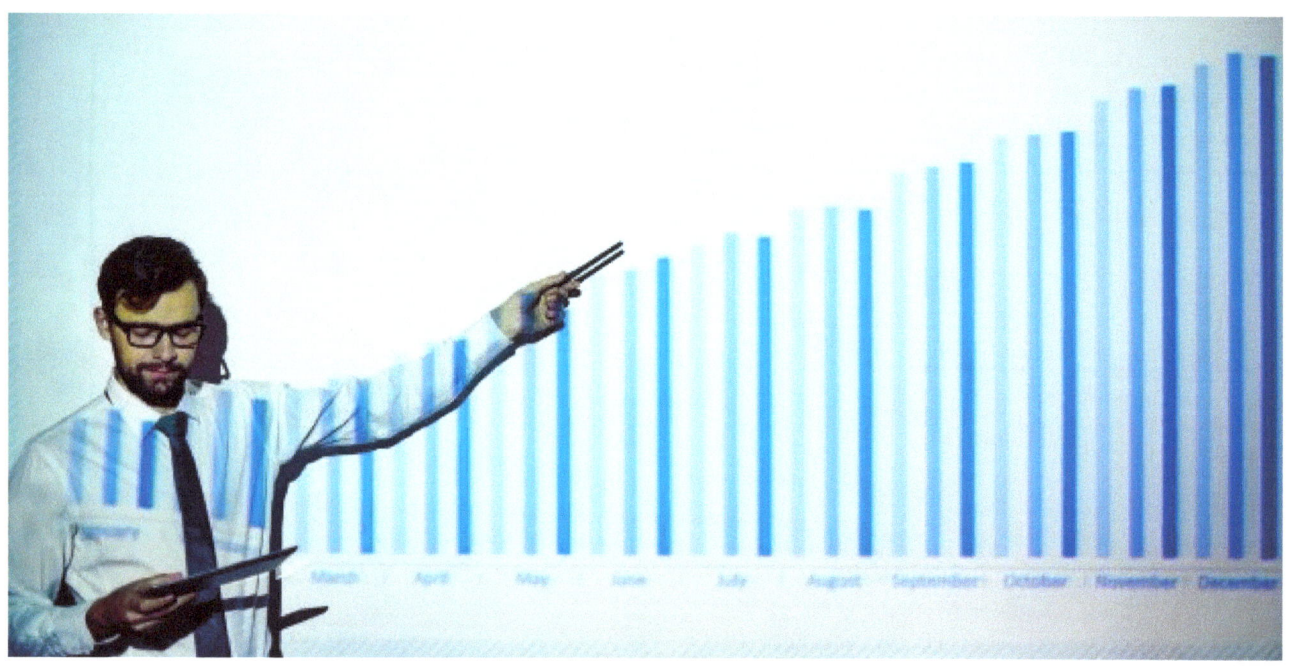

INBOUND MARKETING TACTICS

At this point, you should understand the basic shift in marketing strategies that have occurred due to the emergence of the Internet. Hopefully, you are convinced that you need to take a serious look at inbound marketing for your school. Here are few of the basic tactics involved with inbound marketing so you can better understand what will happen when you adopt an inbound marketing strategy.

SEARCH ENGINE OPTIMIZATION

Abbreviated SEO, these tactics exploit what experts know and can guess from experience about the algorithms that govern internet search engines. While these algorithms are proprietary software, the search engine companies often reveal basic information about what they are looking for from a website. Marketing experts also can give indications based on experience of what works to generate good results. These tactics are directed at computer programs in order to ensure that your website ranks highly for relevant keyword searches.

THE ULTIMATE GUIDE TO SCHOOL MARKETING STRATEGIES

The first step is to develop a buyer persona. These are profiles of the kinds of individuals that you think are good prospects for your school. The buyer persona will help you identify the relevant keywords that you can use in your web design. For example, we saw that Jill and Doug searched for "best Christian schools in Virginia." You can also do keyword research to find out the number of people using specific keywords. This research can indicate the best keywords to use in your site design.

The next step is to integrate those keywords into your website so that the search engines include it in the results for those searches. You can also boost your ranking by maintaining an active web presence through blogging and social media integration. There are many other techniques to attract search engines. Backlinking is the creation of links to your site from other external sites. Search engines like sites with lots of legitimate backlinks. You might also use internal linking within your site and links to authoritative external sites to attract the attention of search engines. Paying attention to these more technical details can help your site rank well on the search engine results page.

A WEBSITE DESIGNED FOR CONVERSION OF TRAFFIC TO PROSPECTS

In our example, Jill and Doug did not follow up with websites that were merely brochures in cyberspace. They were looking for something more. They wanted a site that offered valuable information and could provide solutions to their problems. In addition, they wanted to develop a trusting relationship and a connection with the school itself. SEO tactics attract computers to your school's site. Ultimately, you also need to attract people,

build trusting relationships with them and invite them to take action to solve their problems. This is what a good web design will do; it will convert visitors to prospective families for your school.

The buyer personas you developed for SEO also help here. By understanding whom you are trying to attract and what their problems are, you can design content that solves their problems and builds trust. This trusting relationship can be established through blogging and social media interaction with the visitors to your site. Once this relationship is established, there should be multiple calls to action, or CTA's, within the site. These are invitations to take the next step of downloading an eBook, subscribing to an email newsletter or scheduling a campus visit. Once website visitors, like Jill and Doug, trust that you have their best interests at heart, then they will be willing to exchange some contact information with you. When this happens, you can provide more information about your school and even contact them to invite them to events and to visit the campus.

THE ULTIMATE GUIDE TO SCHOOL MARKETING STRATEGIES

BLOGGING, BUYER PERSONAS, AND STORYTELLING

Blogs are ways to provide an ongoing stream of content that attracts visitors to your site. This content makes your site appear current and authoritative to the search engines. Every time you publish a blog post you are adding a page to your website. This process tied to relevant quality content is rewarded by search engines, like Google; with higher search results it also provides valuable information to the human visitors to your site.

Effective buyer personas are important for determining the topics that you will want to blog about. A buyer persona is a fictional ideal prospective parent who you desire to enroll at your school.

If you develop a buyer persona for a Christian mother concerned about the education her child is receiving at a secular school, then you could focus posts on how Christian schools overcome some of the problems associated with secular education. You could share stories about students who floundered when enrolled at public school, but flourished at your school.

As you develop more buyer personas, you will generate more ideas for content that you can post on your school blog. Buyer personas are the essential building block for putting a successful content creation system into place.

SOCIAL MEDIA

When we first started looking at Jill and Doug's search for educational options, we mentioned that they might ask their friends for information. Today's parents are connected with many of their friends through social media, like Facebook. Jill and Doug can ask their connections how they approached educational choices and receive valuable input. If some of their friends have students at Virginia Christian Academy, then those friends can share their experiences they have had with the school, and point Jill and Doug to Virginia Christian's social media pages and website.

Social media can also transform your current families into marketing ambassadors. It is a powerful amplified for word of mouth marketing. Say Jill and Doug are friends with Bill and Suzy. Bill and Suzy's son, Peter, attends Virginia

Christian Academy and has recently participated in a successful debate competition through the school. Virginia Christian features this news in their blog and shares it on their social media site. Bill and Suzy, proud parents, then share this post on their social media accounts. Now Jill and Doug are aware of Virginia Christian Academy because they saw the post on Bill and Suzy's Facebook pages. Jill and Doug can click through and find out more about Virginia Christian. Bill and Suzy are doing marketing for Virginia Christian Academy without even realizing it.

PAID SEARCH ADVERTISING

Another inbound marketing tactic, when structured correctly, is paid search advertising. We mentioned before that you could pay to have your site show up more prominently in the search engine results for particular keywords. You can also purchase banner advertisements on websites where you believe that people in your target market will see them. These can be effective ways to generate targeted web traffic to your site. Paid advertising is especially good for limited campaigns or

times of the year when you want more people to see your site. For example, you might launch paid campaigns in the early spring when parents are looking to make decisions about school for the next year.

A special note is needed here addressing paid advertising online. Paid Search advertising and buying email lists can also be guilty of the same methods of traditional marketing when used incorrectly. Paid Search advertising when focused on narrow niches and on providing quality content to an audience searching for specific terms can be very useful. However, Paid Search can also be guilty of spray and pray marketing if you're just trying to disrupt people on the internet through goofy pop ads and tricks. Be sure you do not cross this line as it will hurt your school's brand reputation.

INTEGRATING TRADITIONAL MARKETING WITH INBOUND MARKETING

Inbound marketing should be the main focus of your schools marketing plan. However, that does not mean you should simply abandon traditional marketing tactics. Instead, these tactics should support your inbound marketing. Your direct mailings, outdoor, radio, and television advertising should be used to drive visitors to your website. If you want to purchase a billboard at the local mall, that is fine. Make sure you feature your website prominently and even promote a meaningful ebook. Billboards in my opinion should only be used in unique circumstances for schools. For more on this topic please see my blog discussing billboards. There is still a place for traditional advertising, but it now plays a supporting role to the main focus on inbound marketing.

GETTING STARTED WITH INBOUND MARKETING

Now that you know the basics of inbound marketing, it will be tempting to get out there and start a blog or start sharing content on social media. This would be a mistake. The best first step is to develop a strategy for your inbound marketing that guides organize, and integrates your efforts. If you start with a plan, then you can set yourself up for success. Without a plan, your efforts will not be focused and will not lead to much success.

The basis of your strategy will be the development of a variety of buyer personas that will represent the kinds of people who you believe are good prospects for your school. By identifying the general profiles of your best prospects, you can target these people with your marketing. Then you can develop content that will be attractive to these personas and publish that content in places where your best prospects are going to find it. These personas will guide your choices throughout the planning process.

WHEN TO ASK FOR HELP

You might be wondering if you need to bring in outside help in order to be effective at inbound marketing. If you are already spending a lot of money on traditional forms of advertising, you may as well benefit from bringing in an agency or a consultant to work with you in developing and implementing an inbound marketing strategy. Spending money on expert help will be a better use of your marketing budget than another direct mailing. You will generate more high quality leads for your money when you implement an

effective inbound marketing strategy so there is no reason not to divert part of your marketing budget to bring in experts to help.

If you are at a start-up school with limited resources, you are probably spending very little money on marketing anyway. In some ways, this is good news, for many inbound marketing strategies can be implemented at very low cost. You might want to bring in a consultant to help you to get set up and plan the strategy. Then you can delegate the execution of the strategy to support staff or parent volunteers. You will still have to pay attention to make sure that the process is moving along, but you can keep the costs low in this way until you are generating more revenue and can afford a larger marketing budget.

THE ULTIMATE GUIDE TO SCHOOL MARKETING STRATEGIES

CONCLUSION

Let's close with another story related to our hypothetical example of Virginia Christian Academy. Imagine that William Smith is the Headmaster of Virginia Christian. A few years ago, he spent a lot of time worrying about marketing and admissions. He worried about attracting and retaining enough students at the school to provide sufficient tuition to keep the doors open. He was spending a lot of money on traditional forms of advertising, but it was not resulting in a steady stream of new prospective families to look at the school. Mr. Smith did some searching on the Internet and downloaded a guide to school marketing similar to this one. He educated himself about the latest trends in inbound marketing. Finally, he hired a consultant to help him develop an inbound marketing plan for Virginia Christian Academy.

Mr. Smith worked hard to implement the plan, and after six months, he started to see a small but steady stream of new prospective families coming to look at the school. As he continued in his efforts and followed his plan, this stream of prospects continued to grow. Now, after three years, Mr. Smith does not worry about marketing his school anymore. He has a steady stream of interested families that are attracted by the school's effective web and social media presence. Mr. Smith keeps a watchful eye on the marketing process, but he spends most of his time focusing on the mission of the school: the education of young Christian students.

The story of Virginia Christian Academy can be your story. Inbound marketing strategies have a proven track record for increasing the number of prospective families that you generate each year at a low cost. At Schola Inbound Marketing, we want to help you master this new form of marketing. Contact us for a free marketing consultation where we'll spend some time chatting about your school's particular enrollment needs.

THE ULTIMATE GUIDE TO SCHOOL MARKETING STRATEGIES

© 2017 All Rights Reserved

Schola Inbound Marketing
55 New Rd. Unit J6
Ephrata, PA 17522
www.schoolinboundmarketing.com

THE ULTIMATE GUIDE TO SCHOOL MARKETING STRATEGIES

Published by **Schola Inbound Marketing**